HOW TO LIVE LIKE

AN EGYPTIAN
MUMMY MAKER

Thanks to the creative team:
Senior Editor: Alice Peebles
Consultant: John Haywood
Fact checking: Kate Mitchell
Design: www.collaborate.agency

Hungry Tomato™
A division of Lerner Publishing Group, Inc.
241 First Avenue North
Minneapolis, MN 55401 USA

For reading levels and more information, look up this title at www.lernerbooks.com.

Main body text set in Century Gothic Regular 10/13.
Typeface provided by Monotype Typography.

Library of Congress Cataloging-in-Publication Data

Names: Farndon, John, author. | Campidelli, Maurizio, 1962- illustrator.
Title: How to live like an Egyptian mummy maker / by John Farndon ; illustrated by Maurizio Campidelli.
Description: Minneapolis : Hungry Tomato, 2016. | Includes index.
Identifiers: LCCN 2015043850 (print) | LCCN 2015046011 (ebook) | ISBN 9781512406290 (lb : alk. paper) | ISBN 9781512411645 (pb : alk. paper) | ISBN 9781512409161 (eb pdf)
Subjects: LCSH: Mummies--Egypt--Juvenile literature. | Egypt--Social life and customs—To 332 B.C.—Juvenile literature. | Children—Egypt—Social life and customs—Juvenile literature.
Classification: LCC DT62.M7 F365 2016 (print) | LCC DT62.M7 (ebook) | DDC 393/.30932—dc23
LC record available at http://lccn.loc.gov/2015043850

Manufactured in the United States of America
1 – VP – 7/15/16

HOW TO LIVE LIKE
AN EGYPTIAN
MUMMY MAKER

by John Farndon
Illustrated by Maurizio Campidelli

HUNGRY TOMATO™

contents

Mighty Pharaohs

It's the year 1260BCE, and you've arrived in ancient Egypt, the land of the pharaohs. The pharaohs are the most powerful kings ever, no question! They've been ruling here for two thousand years and to us they're like gods. Right now, the pharaoh is Ramesses the Great—and no one, just NO ONE messes with Ramesses! Our enemies the Hittites tried once, and you can see what happened to THEM in the pictures showing the battle of Kadesh on the temple walls at Karnak. *Ugh!* In fact, the "victory" declared by Ramesses at Kadesh in 1274BCE was really a DRAW! And he later married a Hittite princess (and her sister) to patch up the fight.

My name is Neferu, and I'm going to learn the dark secrets of how to turn dead bodies into mummies that last forever. It's a brilliantly gruesome job, but only the chosen few ever get to do it. So if you want to join me, don't you dare call me a mummy's boy!

Ramesses in his war chariot

Who Were the Ancient Egyptians?

The first Egyptians were nomads who settled beside the River Nile and became farmers. Their great days started about 3100BCE when a king called Narmer the Catfish (don't ask!) joined their lands together and became the first pharaoh. About 170 pharaohs came after and ruled over a civilization that lasted three thousand years! Narmer's son, who became the second pharaoh, was called Aha! So he clearly thought it was a good idea too...

Hittite Empire

Egypt

River Nile

Big Hitters

The Hittites ruled an empire in what is now Turkey and Syria. Ramesses took them on in order to defend his empire's borders, and found them every bit as brave as his own warriors.

WARNING!

Mummy makers get involved in some pretty scary stuff. So if you don't like blood and guts, dark places, and dead bodies that come to life and put a curse on you, shut the book now!

The Big River

To learn mummy making, I'm going to school in the Karnak temple. That means sailing up the Nile all the way to Thebes, our capital city. The great River Nile is jam-packed with boats all the time—but it's used for much more than traffic.

It's really hot and dry here in Egypt—*phew*—and the Nile's water is like our lifeblood. We pipe it away for drinking, washing, and watering the crops. Then late in every summer, the river rises and floods the land, keeping it moist and fertile. Farmers grow wheat and barley (for bread and beer), vegetables, figs, melons, and vines. Without that water, we'd all be dead!

All the way down the Nile there are markers to record the level of the water. They are called nilometers. The most famous is on Elephantine Island in the south. This one is the first to show when the flood is starting and when it will end.

The Nile File

The River Nile winds for almost 1,000 miles (1,600 kilometers) through Egypt, from Semna in the far south to the sea. Everyone lives in the long, narrow green strip of land on either side of the river. Beyond that it's scorching empty desert.

Memphis

Thebes

Thebes is our biggest city. Far to the north lies Memphis, which was the capital long ago. It's where the famous old pyramids of our first pharaohs are.

School on a Giant Scale

My school is in the Karnak temple near our capital city, Thebes. It's a truly awe-inspiring place, the biggest temple in the world ever. Everything is gigantic!

But we've got almost no time to look at it. Our teacher is so tough! We sit on the hard floor, but he has a comfortable chair! He makes us practice writing over and over and over all day long on a wooden board covered in white wipe-clean plaster.

Our writing is hieroglyphics, which uses different picture signs to show different things—and there are more than seven hundred signs to learn. When we're older, we'll write on a kind of paper called *papyrus*, made from reeds that grow in the river. But papyrus is expensive, so we can never, ever make a mistake. . .

Karnakered!

Work started on building the vast assembly of temples at Karnak about seven hundred years before my time—and every pharaoh wanted to add something bigger and better. Ramesses the Great topped it all by completing the Hypostyle Hall, the world's biggest-ever room. It is filled with 134 giant stone pillars, the highest 70 feet (21 meters) tall, and each about 45 feet (14 m) around! At Karnak, there's one temple for the god Amun, one for his wife Mut, and another for his son Khonsu. There are perhaps eighty thousand people working at Karnak now, in Ramesses' time. You don't want to see the lines for the toilets!

World of Words

We Egyptians write everywhere—on walls, statues, jars, and coffins. You name it, we write on it! This script is always hieroglyphs. That's why our temples and tombs are like giant picture books. But on papyrus we often use hieratic script, which is much quicker! This uses combinations of symbols to build up words, as well as pictures.

Egyptian Writing Tools (pens made from reeds and a water pot for moistening red and black ink)

If you miss lessons, you'll be badly beaten with a stick, or be made to copy classic texts.

Gods and Demons

Right now we're learning about the gods. They are watching us all the time, from the moment we are born and all the way into the world where we go when we are dead. There's no hiding from them, and they are very, very scary! There are so many gods, I'll never know all of them. But everyone knows the great Osiris, lord of all life.

The old stories say Osiris was murdered by his nasty brother Set and chopped into fourteen pieces. But then his wife Isis used magic to put the pieces back together and bring Osiris back to life. She needed the help of the dog-headed god Anubis, though, which is why Anubis is so special for us mummy makers. All the same, Osiris had to stay in the Underworld, and it became his job to help the dead get born again, which is why he's often pictured wrapped in mummy's bandages. Weird!

Gallery of the Gods

The best-known of our two thousand gods...

Ra: the hawk god, mighty god of the sun

Osiris: god of the afterlife and the dead

Isis: goddess of nature and magic

Horus: god of the sky, war, and hunting

Anubis: protector of the dead and mummy makers

Sobek: the crocodile god, god of water

Thoth: god of magic and sciences

Hathor: goddess of love, beauty, and happiness

Amun: king of the gods, often fused with Ra

Set: god of storms, desert, chaos, and war

The Ankh

The Son's Revenge

Isis and Osiris had a son called Horus, who fought a terrible battle with Set to avenge his father. Horus won, and became the king of Egypt. His spirit lives on in every pharaoh. In the fight, Horus lost an eye, but the god Thoth healed it. This is why the Eye of Horus is a sign of good health and protection. Sailors often paint one on their boats.

Get Ready to Die!

Most Egyptians die young. Perhaps that's why we're obsessed with finding ways to help us live on in the next world. This is where mummy makers come in. You'll need your body in the next world to provide a home for your twin spirits: ka and ba. Ka is your spirit double. Ba is the life force that perches on your body like a bird.

But even if we mummy makers keep your body in one piece, your ba still has to make a long and dangerous journey, passing many tricky tests. Finally, your heart will be weighed in the scales by Anubis to see if it's good and true. If not—it's curtains for you.

Light as a Feather...

If you make it to the Place of Judgment, you'll have to face forty-two judges and swear to them all the sins you have avoided. Then the dog-headed god Anubis will lay your heart in the scales. Only if your heart is as light as Ma'at, the feather of truth, will you be allowed to join everyone in the next world.

The Book of the Dead

If you're traveling to the next world, you need a good guide book to help you avoid the pitfalls. It's called the *Book of the Dead* and it is equipped with all the magic spells you need to help you make it through. We can drop it as a scroll in your coffin, or we can write it all over your bandages, so the spells are nice and handy when you come to a tricky spot. They might even read themselves out if you're not up to it, being a corpse...

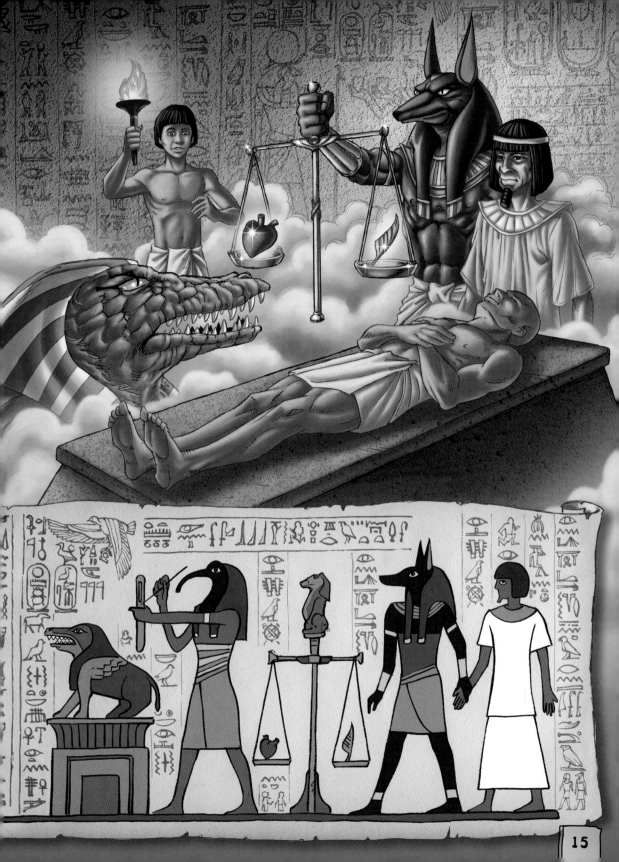

The Embalmer's Secrets

I've finished school, and now I'm about to become a trainee embalmer! Not many people get to do that! Embalmers look after you in the next life, so it's a top job. It's also very, very hush-hush. Mummy making costs a fortune, so only the pharaoh and his family and the richest people become mummies.

We're in a totally secret part of the temple called the *wabet*—and there on the slab in front of us is my first body. It's late at night, so it's seriously scary. Our little team is huddled round the corpse in silence as the priest begins to chant spells. Suddenly, the lamps are blown out, the door opens and in through the shadows strides a man with a huge dog's head. I let out a silent scream! It's the Overseer of Mysteries. He raises his arms and we begin. . .

Let's take you on the journey you'll make when it's your turn to be a mummy! We start by stripping your body of all the soft parts that might rot.

1 Hery Seshta, the Overseer of Mysteries, covers your head with a linen cloth.

3 Parascites the Ripper makes a deep cut in the left side of your body for removing the guts. This so offends the gods, that we then chase him from the room!

2 Sesh the Scribe marks the places on your body where it is to be cut.

4 Wetyu the Bandager takes out your insides, including your lungs and stomach. He leaves your heart, because this will be judged in the next world.

Embalmer's Tools

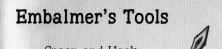

Spoon and Hook: for removing the brain

Ripper's Knives

Funnel for Draining Organs

5 Wetyu Two uses long hooks and spoons to pull your brain out through the nose, bit by bit. Ughh!

6 Hery Heb the priest chants magic spells.

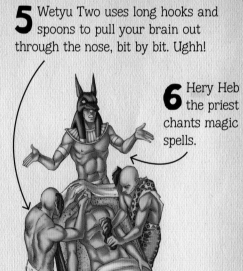

Canopic Jars

We have to wrap your removed innards carefully in linen and store them in four special jars. They're called canopic jars, and each is slightly different.

Hapy the baboon guards your lungs

Duamutef the jackal guards your stomach

Qebehsenuef the falcon guards your guts

Imsety the human guards your liver

Stopping the Rot

Now we have to scrub your body to get rid of any nasty bits, outside and in, everywhere—and I mean everywhere. . . *Yuk!* I hated this at first! But now I really enjoy it—it's a vital part of getting you ready for your great journey.

When your body is quite clean, we lay it in a trough and pack it with a special salt called *natron*. The salt draws out moisture to stop it rotting. After a month, your body is bone dry. And then it's time for the most secret process of all—applying our special recipe of embalming oils! Finally, we stuff the body with sawdust to make it a proper shape again and replace the eyes with pickled onions.Maybe that's why onions make your eyes water. . .

Why Call Them Mummies?

After a few thousand years, the embalming oils ooze out of the bandages and turn into a black and sticky mess that looks rather like tar. When the Arabs came to Egypt in the seventh century, they ransacked the tombs and found these bodies that seemed to be covered in tar. They called them *mumiya*, from the Persian word for tar. The name stuck.

Mummy Recipe

I'm not going to tell you our full mummy recipe. It's a dark secret. But here are some of the ingredients...

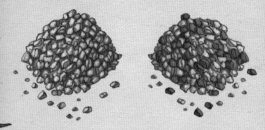

Frankincense and Myrrh (tree resins): to perfume the body

Molten Resin: to fill the body cavities

Sawdust: to stuff the body and give it shape

Palm Wine: to keep the body clean

Wrapping Your Mummy

Now the preservation work is complete, but your mummy still looks a real mess. So we need to give you a beauty makeover. You wouldn't want to go through your whole afterlife—and turn up before Anubis—looking a fright! So we massage your mummy with oils, paint your cheeks, pad out your shoulders, and add eyeliner and hair extensions. Then we seal the slit in your side with a metal plate carved with the Eye of Horus for protection. And finally we begin to wrap you in bandages.

It's a Wrap!

A mummy needs a lot of wrapping. It takes fifteen days to complete the process. And we need about 4,000 square feet (375 square meters) of linen —enough to cover more than one and a half tennis courts. Linen is expensive, so you'll need to save up all your life for your mummy day—unless you're the pharaoh, of course.

The priest reads out spells to protect the mummy in the afterlife.

After we've entirely wrapped the mummy with bandages, I place a pouch of protective charms on the chest.

We lay protective amulets and wrap the mummy in a shroud.

Death Mask

With your mummy fully wrapped, we make a plaster mask to cover your face. We paint it to look like your face (only better), so your ka and ba spirits will recognize you if you're a bit messed up.

You're Not Getting Out Alive!

To give your mummy ultimate protection, we enclose it in a human-shaped wooden coffin. We put that coffin inside another coffin. The second coffin goes in a third coffin, like Russian dolls. And, just for extra insurance, we cover this coffin in magic markings. Then we place them inside a sarcophagus.

Magic Markings

We apply more resin to stick the cloth together. Finally we tie it together with straps and cover the entire body with a sheet.

The Big Day

Two months ago, the great Ramesses died. A sad time for Egypt. But for me it's very exciting! Ramesses ruled for so long that there hasn't been a pharaoh to mummify for sixty-six years. Now I am the Overseer of Mysteries, so—I have the task of embalming him!

I have been working with my team day and night to make sure Ramesses makes the best mummy ever. And we are pleased with our handiwork. He looked almost alive when we began wrapping the bandages two weeks ago. Yesterday we performed the Opening of the Mouth Ceremony, and today we laid Ramesses in his coffin for the final journey to his tomb.

The Opening of the Mouth

Last night, we carried Ramesses' mummy to the temple in secret. I wore my dog-mask as Anubis and held the mummy upright. A priest touched his hands, feet, eyes, and ears with a tool called an *adze*, and opened the mummy's nose and mouth so that he can breathe, eat, and speak in the next world.

The Funeral Procession

In the old days, pharaohs were entombed in pyramids. Now we carry the coffin over the river to the Temple of Amun-Ra in Karnak. The funeral procession will pause for prayers in the Hypostyle Hall. Then we will leave the crowds behind and wind up into the Valley of the Kings, the great cleft in the hills where many pharaohs are already buried. Only the select few will follow Ramesses on this part of his journey—including me.

Going Down!

Workmen have been building Ramesses' tomb for many years now. Yet no one else knows what they have created. Today, though, we will see it for the first and only time.

The entrance to the tomb that will hold the great pharaoh is just a narrow slot in the hillside, which will later be entirely covered to conceal its whereabouts from grave robbers. Just outside we have a final meal to celebrate the start of Ramesses' new journey. Then we lift the coffin and walk fearfully down into the dark depths of the hillside.

Down, down, down we wind, through dark passages carved out of the rock. Flaming torches light our way through the dimness. But we are all utterly silent. Finally, deep underground we reach the burial room where Ramesses' mummy will lie.

Into the Deep

Ramesses's burial room is mind-blowing! Every wall is covered in colorful hieroglyphs telling the story of his life and the pharaoh's great history. But just look at the floor! It's piled high with everything he will need for the next world, and a great pharaoh like Ramesses needs a LOT! Just at a glance I can see mummy-like statuettes called *ushabti* to act as servants; food and wine; and jewels and furniture. He'll live on in style!

The Point of Death

Long ago, the pharaohs' tombs were pyramids—huge, triangular mounds of stone blocks built in the desert. The pharaoh Djoser's pyramid was the first, built some 1,400 years before the time of Ramesses, in about 2650BCE. But none have been built for centuries now. There are mountains all around us in Thebes, so there's no need!

Keeping It Secret

Of the many hundreds of tombs built for the pharaohs, only one ever lasted into modern times—that of the boy king Tutankhamun, whose fabulous tomb was discovered in 1922.

Burying lots of jewels, gold, and other expensive items is just asking for trouble from robbers!

We try to equip the tomb with ingenious secret traps and dead ends to thwart robbers. We even write terrible warnings on the tomb that threaten intruders with all kinds of nasty punishments! But grave robbers are a determined bunch. Very few pharaohs' tombs ever survive intact.

The Last Call

It's finally time to say goodbye to Ramesses. We're lowering his coffin into its home and then we'll seal the tomb. In the old days, servants had to be sealed in the tomb with the pharaoh. Nowadays, we just leave little statues called *shabtis*. The word "shabti" means "one who answers'." A shabti can be brought to life with powerful spells when needed.

The greatest pyramid of them all, that of the pharaoh Khufu (see cutaway illustration below), was built between 2560 and 2540BCE. It is packed full of mysteries. There are many dead ends and secret passages that no one can explain. Some experts think the room believed to be the king's tomb is empty because it was robbed long ago. Others believe Khufu's real resting place was so well-hidden it has not been found.

The empty King's Chamber is thought to be where Khufu was entombed. But was it really a decoy?

Huge stone blocks were released from the Grand Gallery to block the entrance for good. The men who released them exited down the narrow escape route.

No one is sure what these strange tiers of giant stone slabs were for.

Was the Queen's Chamber also a decoy, with the real tomb hidden beneath?

WARNING!

A crushed human skeleton was found in the pyramid of Queen Khamerernebty II beneath a massive stone. Was this a booby trap that caught a grave robber?

Ramesses Rises

Well, we finally helped Ramesses' mummy to embark safely on its journey into the next world. But it wasn't long before grave robbers broke in and stole all the precious things assembled for his journey. So, over the next few centuries, priests secretly moved his mummy from tomb to tomb, until it ended up with many other rescued pharaohs' mummies in a tomb under the temple of Queen Hatshepsut.

I reckon we did a pretty good job mummifying Ramesses, though. You can go to the museum in Cairo and see him there yourself. He still looks pretty life-like—though perhaps a little skinny—over three thousand years after he died! He's not quite as scary as he was in real life. . . or is he?

Microscopic examination of the hair on Ramesses's head shows he was a redhead.

Ramesses' burial chamber was looted and then badly damaged by flooding long ago. But the tomb of his first queen, Nefertari, survives to this day and reveals what his might have looked like. An elaborate series of dark passageways lead down to a suite of huge rooms deep underground, with walls richly painted in hieroglyphs, making it look like a glamorous night club...

In 1974, Ramesses' mummy was taken to Paris to be examined, because it was suddenly beginning to decay. For the journey he was given an Egyptian passport and his occupation was listed as "King (deceased)."

Ten Murky Mummy Facts

1 Embalmers sometimes worked in tents in the open air because the smell of rotting flesh was so horrible!

2 To remove the brains, they chiseled into the nose, then hooked it out bit by bit with a long spoon.

3 Sometimes, embalmers stuffed mud and animal fat under the skin to make a corpse look nice and plump.

4 Animals were often mummified —not just ordinary pets like cats and dogs, but birds, shrews, snakes, and even crocodiles!

5 Mummified cats were sometimes sold outside the temples for people to leave as offerings to the gods.

6 Some people wanted mummified apples, pears, and bits of meat, glazed to look just-roasted, so they wouldn't get hungry in the afterlife.

7 The boy king Tutankhamun's nurse had the mummy of a lion in her tomb.

8 Egyptians believed the flesh of the sun god Ra was pure gold, so they covered the mummies of pharaohs in gold, too, becase they saw them as godlike.

9 A body had to be complete for its journey into the afterlife. So if bits were missing, they added wooden legs, hair extensions, false eyebrows, and a scarab amulet for a lost heart.

10 One careless mummy team lost a lady's internal organs, so they replaced them with guts made of rope, a liver made of cow skin, and kidneys made from rags. Shoddy!

Glossary

ba:
one of your twin spirits: your life force

hieratic:
system for writing with pen on papyrus using symbols to build up words

hieroglyphics:
official writing painted and carved on walls in tombs and temples using pictures to represent things

ka:
one of your twin spirits: your spirit double

mummy:
the preserved remains of a dead person or animal

nilometer:
marker for showing just how high the water in the River Nile has risen during its flooding phase

papyrus:
a kind of paper made from the papyrus reed

pharaoh:
a ruler of ancient Egypt, who had a godlike status

pyramid:
a huge, four-sided triangular mound built as a pharaoh's tomb

sarcophagus:
a carved stone box for housing a coffin

shabti:
little statues placed in your tomb to help you in the afterlife

INDEX

The Author

John Farndon is Royal Literary Fellow at Anglia Ruskin University in Cambridge, United Kingdom, and the author of a huge number of books for adults and children on science and nature, including international best-sellers. He has been shortlisted four times for the Royal Society's Young People's Book Prize.

The Artist

Maurizio Campidelli trained as a graphic designer and illustrator. He has taught illustration and exhibited his own work in Paris, Milan, and Taiwan. He lives in Rimini on Italy's Adriatic coast, where he became involved with comic books. Since 2000, he has worked in computer graphics in many styles, but his personal favorite is a realistic style.